Persephone Blues

ARROWSMITH
PRESS

Persephone Blues
Oksana Lutsyshyna
© 2019 Oksana Lutsyshyna
All Rights Reserved

ISBN: 978-1-7376156-8-2

Boston — New York — San Francisco — Baghadad
San Juan — Kyiv — Istanbul — Santiago, Chile
Beijing — Paris — London — Cairo — Madrid
Milan — Melbourne — Jerusalem — Darfur

11 Chestnut St.
Medford, MA 0215
arrowsmithpress@gmail.com
www.arrowsmithpress.com

Designed by Nicholas Snow

Cover Image by Adriyana Dovha
Lviv, Ukraine

Persephone Blues

by

Oksana Lutsyshyna

CONTENTS

Persephone Blues / 1

yevhen and viktor are in uniforms / 2

I'm lucky my parents were peasants / 3

my grandma Kateryna / 5

The Cat / 7

eastern europe is a pit of death... / 8

a special operation: they shot them all / 9

the conquistador wakes up in the dark / 11

All experience is a means of entombment / 12

I Hear America Singing / 13

My Friend Stefan / 14

A Man and a Woman Get a Cat / 15

Red River Street / 16

generation facebook / 17

a nocturnal animal, I weep / 18

Priscilla / 19

Zero Gravity / 20

...how beauty suddenly blooms near the poorest of houses / 21

Persephone Blues

Demeter wakes early, looks at the sunrise
sees the way the gold spreads into the green of the sea
sees far, all the way to the horizon
sees hungry birds and hard-working fisherman
sees the sandy bottom
sees the underwater rocks and reefs

it turns to day and Demeter and Kora run into each other
like wine flowing from carafe to carafe
they have the same thoughts, same feelings, same desires
same language and same mathematics
in which the simple common denominator is "to be together"

…and close to nightfall, during their last activity
the last dinner by the darkened bay
when it's already impossible to discern between the sea, sky, and earth
they listen to music in a certain restaurant

Persephone blues, Persephone blues, the singer belts out in an unknown language,
Persephone blues, he repeats, as if he wants to remind everyone of something
What is he saying? asks Kora.
What does it matter? says Demeter. The main thing is that we're together.

***

yevhen and viktor are in uniform
in the yellowed photo
the war had just begun
and they smiled because they were young
and the war had just begun – they couldn't
be killed immediately
at the very beginning!..

...the war ended and yevhen was killed
I think he was burned in a tank
but no one knows for sure
but viktor survived and lived a long life
having children and grandchildren and even great-grandchildren
in his last years he feared death
that would soon befall his gray head
his gray body
death he pleaded with death
don't come for me don't come
for my neighbor – because when I see
them carry out his wcasket
I know I'll be next

and young death in uniform smiled
and said – don't be afraid of anything
yevhen will recognize you even gray
from now on no war no photograph

will separate you

***

I'm lucky my parents were peasants
sturdy stock and stout bones
had they been like me, they wouldn't have made it
had they been like me, I wouldn't be here

on roads where ashes roil with dust
where bodies bloom in the rain
where the dead blossom of youth
froze for days, and for a few hours

no one was old
the world was all wounded youths
why did my grandparents survive, why?
was it because they felt the burden of generations

of the unborn, of those to come
in five, in thirty, in fifty years?
...and those who died, they were like
pruned branches, light and free

...and only on my father's side
the cancer of legacy
women's tears like women's fists
proud heads which always fall first

these were women unused to standing for long
because the veins on their legs exploded
who were unable to weep long hours
without going blind, or mad

you had to know how to do everything
tend wounds bake bread dig trenches
nobody taught them
they had to learn for themselves

and they wrote poems - not like before
shorter now, nearly wordless
because they no longer had metaphors
only the clay and the sun

***

my grandma Kateryna
mowed the lawn everyday for the rabbits
danced everyday in the kitchen and in the garden
and still went to work as a guard

watching over some kind of factory
and during her night shifts embroidered towels and napkins
you couldn't scare her – when my grandpa
locked the gates and doors yelling –

go sleep in the street
she took out a secret ladder and climbed into the house through the window
waited in the garden
alone among the sleepy plants

my grandma Kateryna
carried such big love
that when that love surfaced –
totalarian regimes scrambled every which way

the no good drunk men
all kinds of dirt and uncleanliness
it's not a joke that fear itself fell down being afraid
the pots in the kitchen became still

the air brightened
the curtains swayed in the wind
so the neighbors were amazed – how can this be
an ordinary life for an ordinary woman

this Kateryna can do anything
the Lord God speaks with her voice!..
when she was dying
she didn't ask – what's next

she only asked – how are my children
will my children be without a mother?
...and even now the only place in the world
where I am not afraid to be –

is in her presence
even if only in memories
(this Kateryna can do anything
Lord God speaks in her voice)

The Cat

father asked: write a poem about me
how I was young, how I was, period
played the guitar, chased a soccer ball in the field,
bouncing it with my head high into the sky

how I returned home
to our apartment
that smelled of oatmeal and Saturday laundry
with a tapestry hanging on the wall

(on the tapestry
a man and a woman
woven in red
ride a pair of black horses)

no, father, I kept saying, I can't
I don't know how to write about it
it's too close
it's too close, and so it doesn't seem real

alright, he sighed, and went to work
exchanged his fedora for a baseball hat
his guitar for a church choir and soccer for a car
nobody cooked oatmeal anymore, but the tapestry stayed

and then he stopped asking
he realized that I'll never write about him
but we have a cat, he chuckled
write about a cat
a red cat with white spots
a red cat with a white voice
if I don't make it into your writing, at least let the cat remain
woven out of air

eastern europe is a pit of death...

eastern europe is a pit of death and decaying plums
I hide from it in the body of america
but sooner or later I'll slip from this light
back down into that other
and will start talking about death because that is our national sport
talking about death
sad yet beautiful
hoping that the world will hear us and gasp at the beauty and sadness

my lover spreads my fingers with his own
he was educated in good old france
then america
he also studied buddhism and erotica somewhere near the borders
                                                                           of thailand
it's good to drink wine with him and chat
but not about death or eastern europe
because the world's a shithole and it's worthwhile to learn only one art:
that of hopping from one pleasure islet to another
and not giving a damn about plague-infected continents with their
                                                             corpse-eating flies

he kisses me goodnight and disappears into his dream
as I lie in mine, full of summer sun and ephemeral sweetness
mitteleuropa zbigniew herbert whispers in my ear
middle europe enters a labyrinth without a single turn
a labyrinth of fate and freshly laid brick
it enters and doesn't exit
it endures and revives, small like newly seeded grass in the evening
strong like the grandchildren of those that survived the war
when, when will I die? — someone asks in my still childish voice
but I don't hear the answer because it suddenly becomes dark
in this death pit, where miklós radnóti is writing his last poem

***

a special operation: they shot them all
no one was left, and you return
to the house, and see – they are no more.
only their bodies are left,
and you think – where should you go now?
and whom should you ask and about what, if the floor is covered with puddles
that do not heal
and the warmth of blood
evaporates?..

outside you see the empty streets the empty city
people are hiding somewhere in its cracks
but no one can help you
and you think (because now
you can see the past and the future), could I at least
peek at the screen and google
but I have no screen yet
it has not yet been invented

and you think, all right
I am just a part of evolution
ahead of me there are millions of unknown years
behind me also millions
and also unknown

and you see with this new vision
how the waters of the Paleozoic era boil
how in the Permian period ninety per cent of species die out

but no, you realize, they died out slowly
over a span of ten thousand years
this is the standard timeframe
somebody puts a list in front of God
and God approves it

the ten thousandth ones, the losers, their time already going backwards
my species also may not survive
maybe it was already doomed
maybe this is the end of the ten thousand -
the three million six hundred and fiftieth day

of love and geology

***

the conquistador wakes up in the dark
reaches for a candle
lights it

recalls how God showed Himself
as a burning bush

my Lord, he asked, where do You want me to sail
through the darkness
through the thickness of water

the Lord was silent but the ship replied with a moan
one hundred tons
one hundred trees
one hundred nails in its flesh

the water in the ports, its dense odor
and yet, its shallow mirror brings comfort:
soon we will leave this earth
soon we will forget its chronic sorrows

the conquistador lies without his armor
sleepless in his cabin,
where he and his God
the Lord Jesus Christ
are the only light in the dark night

none of them is getting off the boat in this port
no one is leaving the cabin
too small for two

***

All experience is a means of entombment
in an ivory tower, in the hole of the ages,
in a building with a green fence,
in the square of an old foundation.

Give me a crumb of you,
A handful of you.
There is less and less joy in you,
You almost never react to me.

You say: this is the end, or
This is the beginning of the end, or the past,
Where there is laughter, where you pour tea to the top,
And have a second, a tenth serving of dessert.

I Hear America Singing

i hear america singing
her mountain spines and her tunnel hollows
her silent highways
her pointed southern gothic
her flies that hover over the bodies of the dead
her dark oceans and her seas of green weeds

i hear america singing
her religious fanatics
and her fanatics that battle fanaticism
that lone wolf chomsky
and the millions of lone wolves
who come out for the hunt

i hear america singing
her workers, her hoodlums
and her hollywood stars
I hear the song of America sung
by bankers and criminals
and the ever-hungry young

a band plays on the overnight
greyhound bus that churns up the mud
the fingers of the musicians
make the strings blaze
fingers that know everything about me
about me and my own song of america

My Friend Stefan…

My friend Stefan in the corduroy jacket is taking selfies
with the various women who are buying his book
he's all smiles and so are they, happy to have caught him for a short eternity.
I am going over my notes in a coffee shop and crying. My daughter
stayed with me over the weekend; she is so big and independent,
yet I still have no idea what motherhood tastes like.
My roommate Diana is lying on her bed watching Dexter, from time to time
returning to her linguistics homework. She asks me, "native language,
what's it for you?" and I answer,
"It's a house with no room for darkness."
Portland and Tampa and New York and all other cities big and little are but
containers of air filled with the past, those sealed Edens of memory.
Last night I dreamt I learned physics and chemistry and all the other sciences
and now I know all there is to know about every atom
they dance before my eyes and I explain each of their movements with
some law of the universe,
but, knowing everything, I cannot stop believing in god.

***

A man and a woman get a cat,
pet him in the evenings and smile.
They used to smile before, too.
But now the smiles are deeper.
Something shines through them, quietly and persistently.
Vivaldi, a flash of gems.

Would you hold him a minute, says the woman
and hands the cat over to the man.
He places the cat onto his lap,
jokingly pulls his tail.
The woman recognizes something in the man's face
and he stands under her gaze
all figured out.

Like a mountain, in its entrails
another mountain.

Red River Street

there comes a time when Red River Street stops you
stops your car like a red thread that ran out years ago
and you clench the steering wheel and think –
on the left side of the street are apartment buildings
two happy couples once lived there but now have parted
and on the right side is a hospital
where the man you loved was treated
and it seems got well –
the opposite of what happened to you

and you think, how did it happen
that you became a mill in the middle of the desert
and you grind sand with blood
or blood with sand
so that swallowing is easier

on the eve of spring the unwelcome day comes
when you park your car
park but don't get out
they say that maniacs find their prey in women
who don't get out of cars
who sit and write messages to someone
who sit and write grocery lists
or just sit
enveloped by emptiness

Red River Street Red River
finally flood
drown this place
on which we don't fit

generation facebook

the woman writes to him – come back
come back quickly, wherever you are
you are not among the prisoners
not among the fallen
but you are somewhere
maybe you are hiding in the occupied city
but you will get out
come back, come back quickly

she writes and everyone reads
everyone reads and no one can do anything to help
they read about her hope and his death
they read and they cannot do anything to help

what will we remember after this war?
that we shared pain but was it really shared?
or maybe it was,
like a candle that lights up other candles,
it lit up our screens

shared but not eased

***

a nocturnal animal, I weep
over the other animal
because each animal weeps over the other animal
over their warm body

and this weeping cannot be translated into the language
of music
or the language of language:
but only into the language of pilgrimage.

we march on, the animal kingdom,
we are powerful like the reincarnated gods
we have come
to shout into the skies and to ask the stars
first together
and then one by one:

has the earth gone empty?..

Priscilla

it's time

oh no but I haven't lived yet
I'm just getting started
can we do this later?

no, they said

now

...we lived in her house
we were homeless for that summer
and she left us the keys

we cleaned up before moving out:
there was lots of dog fur: she had
two golden retrievers

when she died,
somebody took the dogs
her brother sold the house
giving us a porcelain vase as a memento

...I see a dog with the golden fur step out of the dark
not her dog, a different one
beautiful,
as if from a medieval painting

he steps out of the dark and says something with the human voice
maybe calls her by her name:

Priscilla,

Priscilla

Zero Gravity

on other planets that have zero gravity
we'll live even more eternally than till now
even longer
and even more ephemerally

it's awful to think how much I'd give up
just for one of your tears
ok, for two; or maybe ten,
but I have no treasure to give in return

let me be judged
let me be judged by the grand judge
all of whose tears I've seen
all of whose tears I have

***

...how beauty suddenly blooms near the poorest of houses
maybe a rose, or a cat whose movements enchant you
he walks past the cracked bricks
drinks water from a metal bowl,
looking at you with his young eyes

and somewhere high above his head
a rose is gently rocking on its thin stalk,
as if saying: the Messiah cannot forget about you
because He has no memory

you can either have it all,
or memory –
choose one

and you answer into the emptiness,

though your answer sounds more like a question:
do you want to touch the wound of departing?
do you want to touch the wound of beauty?..

Acknowledgments

Persephone Blues, yevhen and viktor are in uniforms, my grandma Kateryna, the conquistador wakes up in the dark, Red River Street were translated by Olena Jennings

I'm lucky my parents were peasants was translated by Askold Melnyczuk

The Cat and *A Man and a Woman Get a Cat* were translated by Oksana Maksymchuk

a special operation: they shot them all, a nocturnal animal, I weep, Priscilla, how beauty suddenly blooms near the poorest of houses were translated by Oksana Lutsayshyna

eastern europe is a pit of death... and *generation facebook* were translated by Oksana Lutsyshyna and Olena Jennings

All experience is a means of entombment and *Zero Gravity* were translated by Michael Naydan

I Hear America Singing was translated by Virlana Tkacz and Wanda Phipps

My Friend Stefan... was translated by Oksana Lutsyshyna and Ali Kinsella

I'm lucky my parents were peasants was published in English translation in AGNI, Wednesday July 10, 2019.

The Cat was published in Ukrainian in Ukraiński Żurnal/Український журнал, 10/2008; published in English translation in Loch Raven Review, 14.2, 2018

eastern europe is a pit of death... was published in English translation in Words for War: New Poems from Ukraine, an anthology, eds. Oksana Maksymchuk and Max Rosochinsky. Boston: Academic Studies Press. 77-78

All experience is a means of entombment, I Hear America Singing, Zero Gravity were published in Ukrainian in Ja slukhayu pisniu Ameryky (I Am Listening to the Song of America). A collection of poems. Lviv, Ukraine: Old Lion Publishers, 2010.

My Friend Stefan... was published in English translation in New York Elegies: Ukrainian Poems on the City. Ed. by Ostap Kin. Academic Studies Press: Boston, 2018, p. 208

Oksana Lutsyshyna is a Ukrainian writer and poet. She is the author of four books of fiction and four books of poetry, all published in Ukraine. She is currently working as Lecturer in Ukrainian Studies at the University of Texas at Austin, where she teaches Ukrainian language and literature, as well as other Eastern European literatures. She holds a PhD in Comparative Literature from the University of Georgia. She also translates Ukrainian poetry into English in collaboration with the New York-based poet and writer Olena Jennings.

ARROWSMITH is named after the late William Arrowsmith, a renowned classics scholar, literary and film critic. General editor of thirty-three volumes of *The Greek Tragedy in New Translations*, he was also a brilliant translator of Eugenio Montale, Cesare Pavese, and others. Arrowsmith, who taught for years in Boston University's University Professors Program, championed not only the classics and the finest in contemporary literature, he was also passionate about the importance of recognizing the translator's role in bringing the original work to life in a new language.

*Like the arrowsmith who turns his arrows straight and true,
a wise person makes his character straight and true.*

— Buddha

Books by ARROWSMITH PRESS

Girls by Oksana Zabuzhko
Bula Matari/Smasher of Rocks by Tom Sleigh
This Carrying Life by Maureen McLane
Cries of Animal Dying by Lawrence Ferlinghetti
Animals in Wartime by Matiop Wal
Divided Mind by George Scialabba
The Jinn by Amira El-Zein
Bergstein edited by Askold Melnyczuk
Arrow Breaking Apart by Jason Shinder
Beyond Alchemy by Daniel Berrigan
*Conscience, Consequence:
Reflections on Father Daniel Berrigan*
edited by Askold Melnyczuk
Ric's Progress by Donald Hall
Return To The Sea by Etnairis Rivera
translated by Erica Mena
The Kingdom of His Will by Catherine Parnell
Eight Notes from the Blue Angel by Marjana Savka
translated by Askold Melnyczuk
Fifty-Two by Melissa Green
Music In—And On—The Air by Lloyd Schwartz
Magpiety by Melissa Green
Reality Hunger by William Pierce
Soundings edited by Sumita Chakraborty
The Corny Toys by Thomas Sayers Ellis
Black Ops by Martin Edmunds
Museum of Silence by Romeo Oriogun
City of Water by Mitch Manning
Passeggiate by Judith Baumel

www.ingramcontent.com/pod-product-compliance
Lightning Source LLC
Chambersburg PA
CBHW030312100526
44590CB00012B/614